DRAW-AND-TELL

Reading • Writing • Listening
Speaking • Viewing • Shaping

Text and Illustrations
by Richard Thompson

Annick Press Ltd.
Toronto, Ontario

Design and graphic realization
by Monica Charny

Canadian Cataloguing in Publication Data

Thompson, Richard, 1951-
  Draw and tell

ISBN 1-55037-032-4

1. Reading (Elementary) – Language experience
approach. 2. Language arts (Elementary).
I. Title.

LB1573.33.T48 1988   372.4'14   C88-095159-1

Distribution for Canada and the USA:

Firefly Books Ltd.
250 Sparks Avenue
Willowdale, Ontario
M2H 2S4

Printed and bound in Canada
by D.W. Friesen & Sons Ltd.

I would like to dedicate this book to members of the Prince George Storytellers' Roundtable.

I would also like to acknowledge the assistance of Margaret Spicer and Deb Bouska in field testing the stories in their classes and contributing ideas for FURTHER ADVENTURES...

Contents

Foreword 8

Introduction 9

Alexander 13

Banana Cream Pie 19

At the End of the Rainbow 25

Cousin Vladimir 31

Juanita, The Whale 39

The Princess and the Critter 45

The Giant Rabbit Story 51

Trapezoid and Parallelogram 57

Going to Maroonawoo 63

Uncle Bob 69

Katie and the Giant 75

William and Warble 81

FOREWORD

"SKY FULL OF BABIES is a delightfully magical story, but stories for young children are usually written with a lesson in mind. What lesson does SKY FULL OF BABIES teach?" The interviewer was talking about the first of my books for toddlers. I didn't quite know what to say. No one had told me that a story should have a lesson. I thought that magic and delight were more than enough to ask of a story.

Thinking about it, though, I realized that there were lessons in the story, not lessons that I had planned on, but lessons that are inherent in the experience of sharing a story.

I answered, "I hope that SKY FULL OF BABIES will teach children that their ideas, their stories, are valued. I hope it will teach children that language is fun. I hope it will teach them that stories are a magical and delightful thing."

The stories in this collection were also not written with any didactic purpose in mind. My hope is that they will teach at least those lessons. They will also help to enhance listening skills, teach children to recognize and use common language structures in their story telling and writing, help to develop their abilities to read with greater attention, comprehension and recall, develop their confidence and poise in speaking, and provide a vehicle for exploring other language experiences.

Story telling, like many of the best learning media, allows the child to develop and grow from where he or she is now. Whether a child is simply listening to a story, retelling or reworking an existing story or telling a story of his or her own, he or she is participating in a valuable learning experience.

Draw-and-Tell stories are suitable for early primary to junior grades. In using these materials teachers will decide which stories and activities are most appropriate for their class and add ideas of their own.

I think of some of the children with whom I have shared these stories: Justin, age three — He listens attentively to the story and when it is finished says, "Me now!" On a fresh piece of paper he draws circles and circles and circles, retelling the story with complete disregard for the "right" way of doing it. Michael, age four — Every day for a week he asks for the same story. "Do the one about the dragon!" Jesse, age five — She tells the story, BANANA CREAM PIE. You can almost see her checking a mental picture as she draws the figure. She misses a part of the story, but quickly adapts the ending to make it fit. Her monkey is kind of lopsided and has no eyeballs, but she is pleased and so is her audience. Breanne, age eight — She shares a story she has written herself, a draw-and-tell story based on the shape of a Christmas tree. Sam, age eight — The assignment is to choose a book, a story or a poem and do a project based on it. Sam discovers a draw-and-tell story and decides to learn it to tell to the class. He modifies the story a bit, using the names of his friends instead of those the writer has used. In the past, Sam has been shy about presenting material in front of the class, but his story is such a hit with the grade two's that he takes it on a tour of grade one and kindergarten classes. Huy-sun, age twelve — She works with her friend, Jennifer, to learn several draw-and-tell stories. They take turns, one telling the story and the other drawing the pictures. Children in the audience applaud and call out, "Hey, neat! Awesome!"

Whatever the age, grade or skill level of the listener or teller, the single most important thing about story telling is that it is enjoyable, it is fun, it is a delight and it is magical. All other lessons, whatever they may be at different levels, will look after themselves.

RICHARD THOMPSON

USING DRAW-AND-TELL STORIES IN YOUR CLASSROOM
(Early Primary to Junior Grades)

Draw-and-Tell stories can be an effective addition to your collection of Language Arts and Whole Language teaching tools. They are fun to listen to and fun to tell. They are presented in a form in which the structure and pattern of the story is highly visible. Children participate by predicting and anticipating the action. This makes the stories easy to learn and easy to modify and adapt.

The following is an outline of one possible approach for using the stories in your classroom:

Learning the Story
You will probably want to start with one of the stories at the beginning of the book, one that doesn't use extra devices such as flipping the drawing.
— read the story
— draw the figure on a small piece of paper and try to relate key elements in the story to the parts of the drawing
— compare your drawing with the "map" that accompanies the story, noting missing elements
— repeat the last two steps until you have a feeling for the relationship between the story elements and the figure
— try telling the story with the book close at hand for reference. With some draw-and-tell stories you are drawing all or most of the time you are talking. That is not the case with these stories. You will often find yourself telling long passages of the story without referring to the drawing at all
— practise a few times until you can tell the story without the book. You will probably *not* want to learn the story word for word — in fact, the story will be more effective if you have a good grasp of the structure of the story and can feel free to use your own words within that structure
— note the "telling points" that follow each story. The "telling points" are there to alert you to important story elements or to suggest ways to enhance your telling
— practise the story in the actual format that you will use when presenting it to an audience

Telling the Story
Especially when telling to children who have had previous exposure to draw-and-tell stories, you will probably want to admonish them to "keep the secret". Even with such an admonition you will find children waving their hands as they realize what the figure is. Acknowledge that you know that they know with a nod, or by putting your finger to your lips, but try not to interrupt the flow of the story.

Another idea is to establish a signal before you start. "There is a surprise in this story. If you guess the surprise, put your finger on your chin, but keep the secret. I will know that you know, but it must remain *our* secret for now."

Repeat the story another day. Even after they know the secret, children enjoy the story for its own sake. It is partly through repeated tellings that the children will begin to learn the story well enough to attempt a retelling on their own.

Reviewing the Story

Have the children work as a whole group to identify the key points of the story and map them on a completed drawing.

Encourage Retelling

— in partners
— in small groups
— to the class
— to other classes in the school

Have the children work in pairs — one learning the figure, one the story — to present the story as a team.

Encourage the children to think in terms of the structure and pattern of the story. With that in mind, it is probably best to *not* provide the children with a copy of the text of the story. Allow them to reconstruct the story from their knowledge of the structure and pattern and from their memory of their telling. Keep in mind that the process is more important here than the product. Any story is, to a certain extent, created anew with each teller. The version that you tell, and the versions that your students tell again, will all be different from the story I had in mind when I wrote it down. The figure, too, may look different than the one I provided. That is part of what story-telling is about.

Make it an Adventure

The "Further Adventures..." section following each story provides some suggestions for exploring the stories in other ways:
— changing and adding elements
— expanding and rewriting the story within the structure
— doing activities related to the story

The Visual Story

Draw-and-tell stories have a built-in visual "map", but creating a visual model of your story can be a valuable aid to learning, telling and/or writing any kind of story.

— Work with a story you already know, one you are trying to learn to tell or one that you are writing. Draw a picture of the landscape as it unfolds throughout the story. Include details that are not necessarily part of the text or plot of the story. For example, if you are telling THE THREE LITTLE PIGS, draw a picture of the house of straw, but think about where it is — is it by a stream? Is it in the forest? Where is it in relation to the house of sticks? Where is the wolf's den? Include those details in your drawing. Use coloured pencils or markers so that you can see the landscape of your story in colour. Now when you come back to tell your story or work on it some more you can "look around" and see where you are.

— Make a map of a familiar story or a story you have written. This is similar to the idea above, but instead of including a lot of detail, you are going to simplify and use symbols for things. Don't worry about trying to make the finished map look like a picture. Tell the story as a draw-and-tell story (again, it doesn't matter if your drawing doesn't make a recognizable picture).

— Draw a picture of how one character *feels* in the story. Move your pen across the paper as you think of the things that happen in the story. When your character is happy, your pen should go up, and when your character is unhappy, it should go down. Your line will look like a graph or the line on an oscilloscope. It is one other way of "seeing" your story. Do the same thing for each of the characters in the story. Instead of being happy or sad, the character in your story might change in other ways — timid/brave, foolish/wise, hopeful/despairing or evil/good.

Other Materials

A visit to the library in teams of two or small groups will probably yield suitable materials to add the "draw" component to the "tell" story or song. Have the children practise their own "map" of a chosen subject, then transfer it in appropriate stages to the easel, as a partner tells
— a familiar fairytale or other story
— a nursery rhyme or other poem
— a song

Drawing and Telling

a) Have the children invent (not necessarily write), their own story, accompanied by a step-by-step "map", contributed by the author, or the teacher. It is best, of course, if the children do create their own stories. If it proves too difficult initially, a theme might be casually suggested, as in, "Who wants to make up a bicycle/teddy bear/baby sister story?"

b) Have teams of two *begin* a draw-and-tell story, then turn the half finished tale over to another team to complete it.

c) Have children in the classroom take turns contributing a single sentence at a time to an unfolding collective story, with teacher or student volunteer at the easel, composing away at the "map".

Turn the Process Around

RED RIDING HOOD (or GOLDILOCKS AND THE THREE BEARS)

Read the story to the class. Having practised your Wolf, Red Riding Hood or Goldilocks drawing, introduce the title of the fairytale, draw an introductory figure, then invite children to take turns telling parts of the story, helping you along while you draw the map.

Extension: Appoint voices to be "chorus" for "oh ohs!" or "don't do its!" or voices of Red Riding Hood, the Wolf and Grandma, or the Bears and Goldilocks.

I Draw-You-Tell

a) Choose one of the stories in this book, one that is popular with the children in your class. Choose the map, mention the title of the story, and begin by drawing the outline, inviting the children to tell what is happening.

b) Name a favourite story, *any* story the children are familiar with. Explain that you will draw a "map" of the story, but cannot complete it unless helped by the group to supply the story-line. Stop frequently, ask if you should do a circle, a zigzag line or triangle here. Complete story and map together.

Have an "I-Tell-You-Draw" Session

Choose a familiar, popular story. Name the title. Explain that you or a fellow student will tell it slowly. Invite each of the children to draw their individual "map" on their own piece of paper.

The What-On-Earth-is-This? Story

Prepare a large size "map". Attach it to the easel. Inform the class that you have lost the story that goes with it. Could they make one up?

⑥ The tree

⑦ She sees the owl and hears a noise

⑤ The frog is here

③ The pond

⑧ The squirrel

⑩ A doughnut for her

⑪ A doughnut for himself

④ The duck is here

① The balloon

⑫ A great big smile

⑨ Back to where she started

② The butterfly

ALEXANDER

One day, Jesse took Alexander to the park.
    "You wait here," she said. "I'm going to
go and buy a balloon from the balloon man.
    [*This is the balloon she bought.*]

When she got back to where she had left
Alexander, he was gone.
    But there was a butterfly fluttering about
[*this is the butterfly*], and Jesse asked her,
"Do you know where Alexander is?"
    The butterfly shook her antennae and
said, "No, I don't know where Alexander is.
I don't even know WHAT Alexander is."

"You could try asking the Duck. She loves
to gossip, knows everything that's going on
in the park. She lives over by the pond. It's
worth a try."
    [*Jesse walked across the park to the
pond where she found Duck chatting with
some pigeons*.]
    "Do you know where Alexander is?"
Jesse asked.
    "No, my dear, I'm afraid I don't know
where Alexander is," replied the Duck
shaking her beak. "In fact, I don't even
know WHAT Alexander is."

"You might try the Frog who lives on the other side of the pond. I thought I heard him croaking about something a bit earlier."

[*Jesse walked around the pond and found the Frog there practicing one-legged leaps.*]

"Do you know where Alexander is?" Jesse asked.

"Nope!" croaked the Frog, shaking his round green head. "Don't know WHAT Alexander is. Nope!"

"Try owl," croaked the Frog. "Big tree over there."

[*Jesse walked to the other side of the park, where she saw an owl asleep in a big oak tree.*]

"Do you know where Alexander is?" Jesse asked.

The owl didn't answer. He was asleep.

Jesse heard a noise from the other side of the tree.

"Alexander!" she cried.

[*She ran around the tree*.] She found a bushy-tailed squirrel, but no Alexander.

"Do you know where Alexander is?" she asked the squirrel.

"No, no, no!" chattered the squirrel, shaking his tail. "Sorry, sorry, sorry. Don't know where, don't know what!"

[*Jesse walked back to where she had first left Alexander*.]

"Did Alexander come back?" she asked the butterfly, who was still there.

"I didn't see any Alexander," said the butterfly. "But wait here a minute and I will see what I can see."

She fluttered up into the air and back down again.

"There is something coming across the park," she said, "but I don't know if it's an Alexander."

Jesse ran in the direction that the butterfly had pointed.

Sure enough, there was Alexander walking along carrying a paper bag.

"Alexander! Where have you been?" cried Jesse. "I've been looking all over for you!"

"I got us a treat," said Alexander. He reached into the bag and brought out two doughnuts. [*"One for you. And one for me"*]

[*And he smiled a big smile.*]

Jesse is happy that she knows where Alexander is.

Do you know WHAT Alexander is?

TELLING POINTS

1. Keep the secret — don't mention that Alexander is a bear.

2. Each of the animals that Jesse meets reinforces the mystery when he/she says, "I don't even know WHAT an Alexander is."

3. At the end of the story wait for the audience to supply the answer to the question, "What is Alexander?" and then say it yourself... "Alexander is Jesse's teddy bear!"

THE FURTHER ADVENTURES OF ALEXANDER

1. Retell the story using your name and the name of your teddy bear. Think up names for the animals that you meet in the park.

2. Think about the characters that Jesse meets on the way. What kind of voices would they have? Retell the story using different voices and manners of speaking for each of the characters.

3. Retell the story with different animals along the way. What would the animals be doing as Jesse approached?

4. Try the story with different people along the way instead of animals — a policeman, a boy selling ice cream... or your friends perhaps.

5. Maybe the story doesn't take place in a park at all. How would you change the story to make it work if Jesse lost Alexander at the circus? Or on the way to the library? Or at a friend's birthday party?

6. Invite everybody's teddy bear to come and hear you tell the story.

7. Learn the song "Teddy Bears' Picnic".

8. Draw a portrait of your teddy bear.

9. Read TEDDY RABBIT by Kathy Stinson.

10. Make a teddy bear puppet.

11. Have you ever lost anything that was important to you? Write a story or poem to tell how you felt about it.

12. Read SEAL IS LOST by Priscilla Galloway.

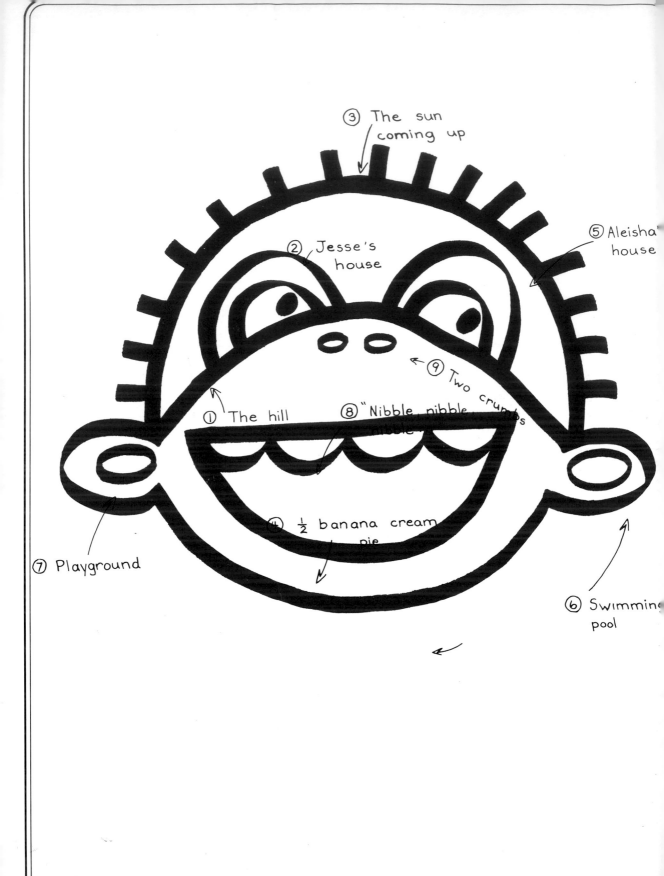

BANANA CREAM PIE

Jesse lived in a little house on Richmond Hill. [*Here's the hill and here's Jesse's little house.*]

One fine morning, when the sun was shining and the birds were singing, Jesse decided to bake a banana cream pie.

Josh wanted to bake, too, but he wasn't much help. He juggled with the bananas and the eggs. He spilled the flour. He walked on the table and knocked over the milk.

Finally, Jesse sent him outside to play and finished the pie herself.

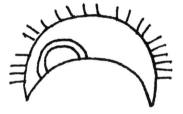

When the pie was cooled, Jesse called Josh, and they sat down together and ate half the pie, just like that.

"Let's take the rest to Katie," suggested Jesse.

Katie was Jesse's best friend...

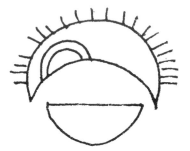

...and she lived right next door.

When they got to Katie's house, the door was open, but no one was home.

"I bet she's at the swimming pool," said Jesse. "Josh, you stay here and wait. I'll go get her and be right back."

She put the banana cream pie on the table and went to look for her friend.

She walked down the hill to the swimming pool. [*This is the swimming pool.*] Jesse walked all around the pool looking for Katie. She wasn't there.

"She must be at the playground," thought Jesse.

[*The playground was quite far away — over here.*]

So...

...Jesse walked all the way around to the playground. She walked around looking for Katie and calling her name.

Finally, she found her near the jungle gym.

"Katie!" called Jesse. "Let's go to your house. I have a surprise for you."

"A surprise!" said Katie. "Let's go!"

"Josh, we're back!" called Jesse.
   But Josh was gone.
   And someone had eaten all the pie —
nibble...nibble...nibble...nibble...

All that was left were two tiny crumbs.
   "Oh, Katie! Josh ate your surprise!" cried
Jesse.
   "What was it?" asked Katie sadly.
   "It was a piece of banana cream pie," said
Jesse.
   "It's okay," said Katie. "Let's make
another one!"

And the lesson of that story is: Never leave a
monkey alone with a banana cream pie.

TELLING POINTS

1. It is fun, when you get to the part about making the banana cream pie, to have the children in the audience help with suggestions of what Jesse and Josh might need to make the pie.

THE FURTHER ADVENTURES OF JESSE AND JOSH

1. Use your name and the names of friends in retelling the story. Feel free to invite any number of other friends from the pool or the playground back to share the surprise.

2. Working alone or in a group, make a list of some places, other than the swimming pool and the playground, where Jesse could look for Katie. Use some of your ideas in a retelling of the story.

3. Add to the search for Katie by adding a body for Josh.

4. Look up the recipe for banana cream pie and share it with the class. Find other banana recipes that might appeal to Josh.

5. With an adult's help, try cooking one of the banana recipes.

6. Do some research to find out what other things monkeys like to eat.

7. Can you think of other stories that feature monkeys? Make a list.

8. Learn another monkey story to share with the class. CAPS FOR SALE by Esphyr Slobodkina might be a good one to start with.

9. Bring your toy monkeys and a banana to school and have a "Monkey Business" day.

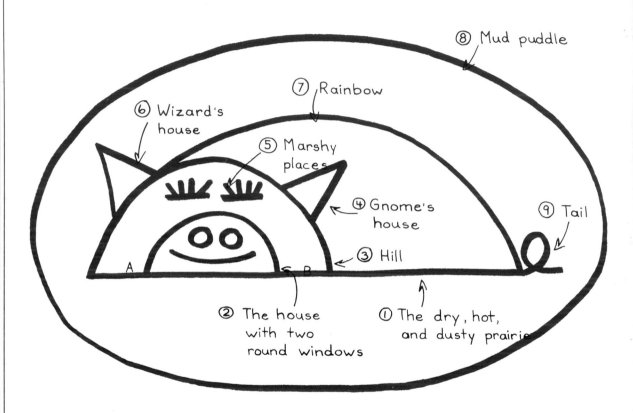

⑧ Mud puddle

⑦ Rainbow

⑥ Wizard's house

⑤ Marshy places

④ Gnome's house

⑨ Tail

A

③ Hill

B

② The house with two round windows

① The dry, hot, and dusty prairie

Note: Length A + B are approximately equal

AT THE END
OF THE RAINBOW

Nicholas lived on the flat, dry, hot and dusty prairie....

...in a little house with two round windows.

One day he looked out the window and saw a beautiful rainbow stretched across the sky behind the hills.

He had heard that there was treasure to be found at the end of the rainbow, so he set out across the arid plain to see if he could find it.

He walked until he came to the hill country. Hot and tired and thirsty, he toiled upward. Eventually, he came to a small hut where a gnome lived.

"How much further to the end of the rainbow?" Nicholas asked the gnome. "I'm looking for the treasure."

"Ah!" said the gnome. "Tell me, friend, what one thing would make you happier than anything else in the world? Perhaps I'll be able to help, and perhaps, I'll not."

Nicholas wiped his forehead and thought for a moment. Then he knew what would make him very happy indeed, and he told the gnome.

"Ah, that's not too much to wish for!" said the gnome. "Go as you've been going, then, past the marshy places, and you will come to the hut where Bunyard lives. Good-bye!"

And so Nicholas set off, trudging up the hill and past the marshy places until...

...he came to a second hut where he met the wizard, Bunyard.

"So tell me, my friend," the wizard said, "what one thing in the world would make you happiest of all? Perhaps I'll be able to help you, and perhaps I'll not."

Nicholas told him. Bunyard laughed.

"That is not so much to wish for!" he said. "Come."

He led Nicholas to the rainbow and gave him a pair of magic boots.

"Up you go!" he said. "If you make it over, you will find...what you will find..."

Nicholas put on the boots and started to climb. He climbed and climbed all day under the hot sun until he reached the top of the rainbow.

He looked down. There at the end of the rainbow was — THE BIGGEST MUD PUDDLE HE HAD EVER SEEN!

With a squeal of delight, he slid down the rainbow and sunk into the cool, delicious mud...

...right up to his tail.

A smile spread across his face. And at that moment, he was the happiest pig in all the world!

TELLING POINTS

1. Remember — DON'T say that Nicholas is a pig until the last line.

2. Be sure to stress the "hot, dry, dusty..." when describing the flat prairie and when telling about Nicholas climbing the hill. This sets the audience up for the surprise of the cool, soothing, wet mud hole at the end.

THE FURTHER ADVENTURES
AT THE END OF THE RAINBOW

1. Make a list of the things "that would make you happier than anything else in the world."

2. Working alone or in a group, make a list of other creatures or magical characters who could live in the two huts on the hill. Pick two to use in retelling of the story.

3. Nicholas' eyes are made by drawing the "two marshy places". Experiment with other shapes for the eyes and think what they might represent in the story.

4. Nicholas was given magic boots to walk up the rainbow. What other device, magical or otherwise, might Nicholas have used to get to the top of the rainbow? Use one of your ideas in the story in place of the magic boots.

5. Often in stories involving quests the person is called upon to answer riddles. Can you think up three riddles — pig riddles maybe — that the gnome or the wizard can require Nicholas to answer?

6. Paint a beautiful rainbow with your own perfect treasure at the end.

7. On your own or working in a group make a list of other pig characters in stories you have read. How do they compare with Nicholas?

8. Organize a "Pig Tales" storytelling session featuring stories or poems about pigs.

9. Write a story, a poem or a song in praise of mud.

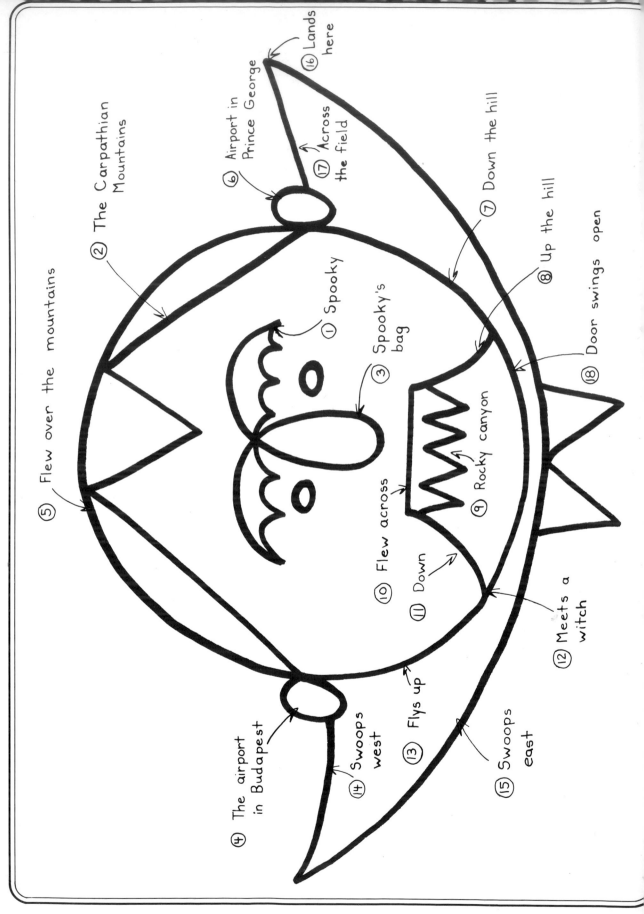

① Spooky
② The Carpathian Mountains
③ Spooky's bag
④ The airport in Budapest
⑤ Flew over the mountains
⑥ Airport in Prince George
⑦ Down the hill
⑧ Up the hill
⑨ Rocky canyon
⑩ Flew across
⑪ Down
⑫ Meets a witch
⑬ Flys up
⑭ Swoops west
⑮ Swoops east
⑯ Lands here
⑰ Across the field
⑱ Door swings open

COUSIN VLADIMIR

This is the story of a bat named, Spooky. [*This is Spooky.*]

Spooky lived far, far away amongst the Carpathian Mountains. [*These are the Carpathian Mountains.*]

Spooky was flapping about in the Carpathian Mountains one night, when he happened to flap past his mailbox. He noticed that there was a letter there for him, and he flapped down excitedly to see who it was from, because Spooky very rarely got letters from anyone. As soon as he saw the postmark — Prince George, B.C., Canada — Spooky knew that the letter was from his cousin, Vladimir. Vladimir was the only person that Spooky knew in Canada.

"Cousin Spooky," the letter read. "We are having a family reunion this year here in Prince George. Please come!" And it was signed "your cousin, Vlad".

Well, Spooky packed his bag then and there. He put in dried worm tongues, pickled rhino horns and marinated frog eyes — party food that he'd been saving for just such an occasion.

Then he started off — flapping, flapping, flapping, flapping, flapping, flapping — through the dark Carpathian night. By dawn he was exhausted, and seeing a man walking on the road below, he swooped down and asked him, "Am I in Prince George, B.C., Canada yet?"

"No," laughed the man, "but you are almost in Budapest. If you want to get to Canada you had better take an airplane. It is a long way to fly."

So Spooky walked to the airport in Budapest. He sent a telegram to his cousin and bought a ticket.

Off he flew, over the mountains and over the sea and finally landed in Prince George.

When he got off the plane, the airport was deserted. Spooky had expected Vladimir to be there to meet him, but there wasn't a soul around. He waited. And he waited.

Spooky had just decided to take the very next plane back to the Carpathian Mountains when the clock began to strike midnight, "Bong! Bong! Bong…"

A strange little gnomish sort of a man scuttled through the door and beckoned to Spooky to follow him.

Outside on the driveway there was a huge black coach pulled by seven spectral horses. The gnome opened the door, Spooky climbed up onto the velvet seat, and the door closed.

A moment later, he could feel the coach moving swiftly down a long hill. Then, all of a sudden, they were going up again, rumbling and bumping over a rough track.

The door opened, and the gnome motioned for Spooky to get down. Then, without a word, he jumped up onto his seat, and whipped up the horses. In a moment, they had disappeared back down the road by which they had come.

Spooky could see that the road dropped away into a canyon full of jagged pinnacles of rock.

Gathering all his strength and clutching his bag in his claws, he flew wearily across the canyon, and landed on the other side.

He walked along a rough path through the forest and sat down to rest.

His head began to nod, and he was almost asleep when he heard a noise behind him.

He turned to see a witch sitting there, grinning her snaggle-toothed grin.

"Come for a ride, dearie!" she cackled. "Climb on my broom and I will take you where you need to go."

What could Spooky do? He climbed onto the broom behind the witch. And then...

ZOOM! They soared to the west...

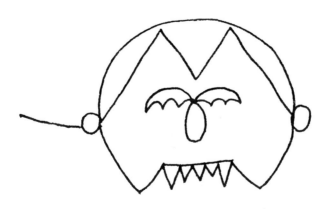

...and turned and swooped back toward the east so fast that Spooky had to clutch onto the broomstick with all his strength to keep from being swept off by the wind.

And then they stopped.

"End of the line, dearie," said the witch. "There's the place you're looking for. Go carefully!"

Spooky started across the field to the hulking dark shape that the witch had shown him.

When he got closer, he saw that it was a massive, rambling house. All the windows were dark. Several were broken. Shutters hung crooked on their hinges. The garden was totally overgrown with weeds.

Spooky walked up the creaking stairs and lifted the heavy knocker.

"BOOM! BOOM! BOOM!" The noise echoed through the house.

A light came on in one of the tower rooms.

There was the sound of footsteps.

The door creaked open. A tall man, dressed all in black, stood there. He held one arm, draped in a black cape across in front of him, hiding all of his face but his eyes. Those eyes stared at the little bat, making a shiver run down his wings. And then...

...all the lights came on. The gnome, and the witch called out, "Surprise!"

And the vampire swept aside his cape and laughed, "Welcome to Prince George, Cousin Spooky! You are just in time for the party!"

TELLING POINTS

1. You will probably want to change the name of the city where Cousin Vlad lives from Prince George to wherever you are.

2. When you draw Spooky, someone is going to yell, "Where's his head?" Press on. You may want to acknowledge that you heard with a nod, a wink or a finger to the lips, but don't stop to explain that this is a symbolic bat.

THE FURTHER ADVENTURES OF SPOOKY

1. Working alone or in a group, make a list of other things that Spooky might want to pack in his bag. What might those things be used for?

2. Draw a picture of Cousin Vlad's house.

3. Working alone or in a group, make a list of other guests who might show up at the family reunion. Draw a picture of the party or individual portraits of the guests.

4. Get together with some friends. Each of you imagine you are a different guest at the party. Start by thinking of a simple message. Speaking in the voice and manner of your character, pass the message to another guest. He or she, speaking in character, passes it along to a third guest and so on until everyone has heard the message. Swap characters and try a different message.

5. Perform some magic. Change the gnome at the airport to some other kind of a creature. Is this creature driving a coach? What then? How about the witch that appears later on — try changing her too.

6. Check out Charlotte Diamond's "Looking For Dracula" on her album 10 CARROT DIAMOND. Learn it and share it with the class.

7. On your own or in a group, make a list of good ghoulish games to play at Cousin Vlad's party.

8. Working alone or in a group, make up the menu for the party.

9. Find out everything you can about vampire bats. Share your information with the rest of the class.

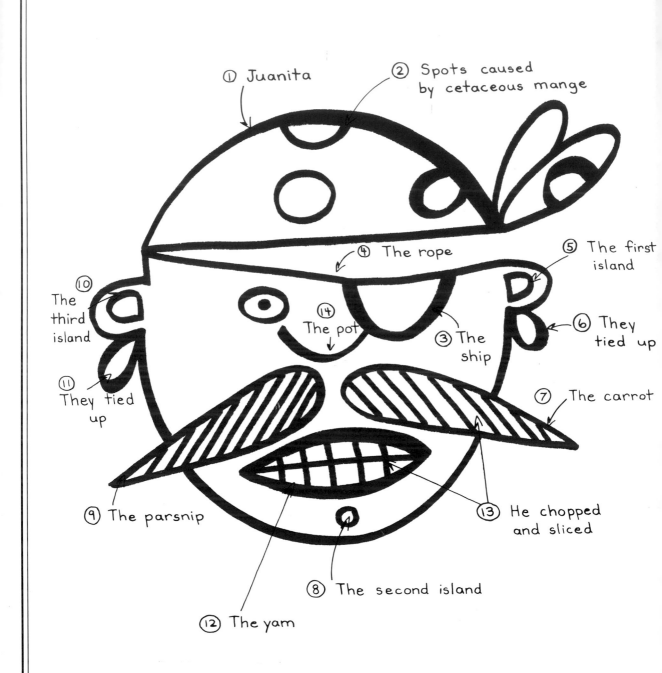

① Juanita
② Spots caused by cetaceous mange
④ The rope
⑤ The first island
⑩ The third island
⑭ The pot
③ The ship
⑥ They tied up
⑪ They tied up
⑦ The carrot
⑨ The parsnip
⑬ He chopped and sliced
⑧ The second island
⑫ The yam

JUANITA, THE WHALE

Juanita was a whale who lived in the Caribbean Sea in a time when pirates roamed the waves. [*This is Juanita swimming along in the sea.*] Juanita had heard about pirates — that they were mean and fearsome — and she wasn't keen to meet one.

So she decided to swim away to another ocean where pirates didn't go. She headed off and had just passed the island of Martinique when...

...her tail stopped working! She couldn't swim another stroke. And that was not all! She looked down and saw that there were great big spots forming on her body.

"Oh dear!" she thought. "What is happening to me!"

She was floating helplessly on the Caribbean Sea, when...

...a ship sailed up close to her side.

"Ahoy, mate!" called a man from the deck of the ship. "It seems you've lost the use of your rudder!"

"Pirate!" thought Juanita. And she said, "Oh, no, I'm fine. I'm just resting."

"Now, girl, you don't be trying to kid me!" said the man, squinting at Juanita with his one good eye. "It so happens I'm a Marine Vet'narian, and it so happens, too, that I can tell a case of the Cetaceous Mange when I sees it!"

"Grab onto this line, girl, and I'll tow yer into Martinique, and I'll be getting some stuff there to fix yer up."

So Juanita held the rope in her jaws and off they sailed.

[*Martinique was a small island right over here.*]   The man sailed his ship around the island and tied up in the port. [*Right here.*]

"I'll be going ashore for a bit," he told Juanita. "Be back in a shake."

While she waited Juanita noticed that there were more spots on her body than there had been before.

A while later, the man came back with a large carrot.

"This is all I could find here," he said. "We'll have to sail on to Grenada to find the other things I'll be needing."

"I see the spots are spreadin'," he said, "but don't yer worry. I'll have yer fixed up in no time."

So they sailed on...

...to the island of Grenada [*way down here.*]

Again the man went ashore, and again, as Juanita lay there waiting, she looked and saw that more spots had formed.

The man returned with a large parsnip.

"Bilge water and barnacles!" he grumbled. "I'm not having much luck. There's not a yam to be had on the whole island. Nothing for it but to head for St. Croix!"

He untied the ship and off they sailed.

St. Croix was a good ways north, [*up here*] and by the time they reached it, Juanita was almost totally covered with spots.

The man tied up the ship and went ashore.

Juanita waited and waited and waited. Finally, the man came back.

"I had a devil of a time finding it, but here it is!"

[*Here it is — the great big yam that he had found.*]

They left the port and sailed around the island.

And as soon as they were in open water, the man went down to the galley. He sliced the carrot. He sliced the parsnip. And he chopped the yam into small pieces.

He put the pieces all in a pot. [*This is the pot...*], put it on the stove and let it cook into a yellowish mush. He added a few secret ingredients and stirred it all around.

Then he scooped up a big ladleful and gave it to Juanita.

"Swallow it down, lass," he said. " 'Tis a sure cure for the Cetaceous Mange!"

Juanita swallowed the medicine, and, as if by magic, the spots started to disappear. And her tail was working again! It was a bit stiff, but she could move it!

"Oh, thank you!" cried Juanita.

"My pleasure," said the man.

"I have to tell you something, though," said Juanita, blushing a bit. "I didn't really believe you when you said you were a Marine Veterinarian."

"Har! Har!" laughed the man. There was a bit of a twinkle in his one good eye. "I suppose you thought I was a pirate!"

"Yes," admitted Juanita. "I did think that."

[*And what would you have thought, if you had seen this man?*]

TELLING POINTS

1. Put in a bit of extra practice getting the carrots and parsnip in the proper position on the figure. When you are drawing the carrot, try to visualize where the nose will be.

2. Remember to add more spots at each stop along the way as Juanita's condition gets worse.

3. Remember — DON'T say the man is a pirate.

THE FURTHER ADVENTURES OF JUANITA, THE WHALE

1. Juanita had heard about pirates. And she was worried about this "vet'narian". Think of some of the stories that Juanita might have heard. If the stories are short, you might want to weave them into the draw-and-tell by telling what Juanita was thinking as she waited for the man to return to the ship each time.

2. There are many islands in the Caribbean Sea. Look in an atlas and find other names that could be used for the islands that they visit.

3. Think up some other names for the disease that Juanita has.

4. Write the recipe, including the secret ingredients and the method of preparation, for the "medicine".

5. Practice telling the story using a "pirate's voice" for the man.

6. Draw a picture of the vet'narian's ship.

7. Visit the library. Find out the names of some real pirates from long ago. Also look for *books* on pirates.

8. Look for other stories about whales.

9. Make a classroom mural on whales.

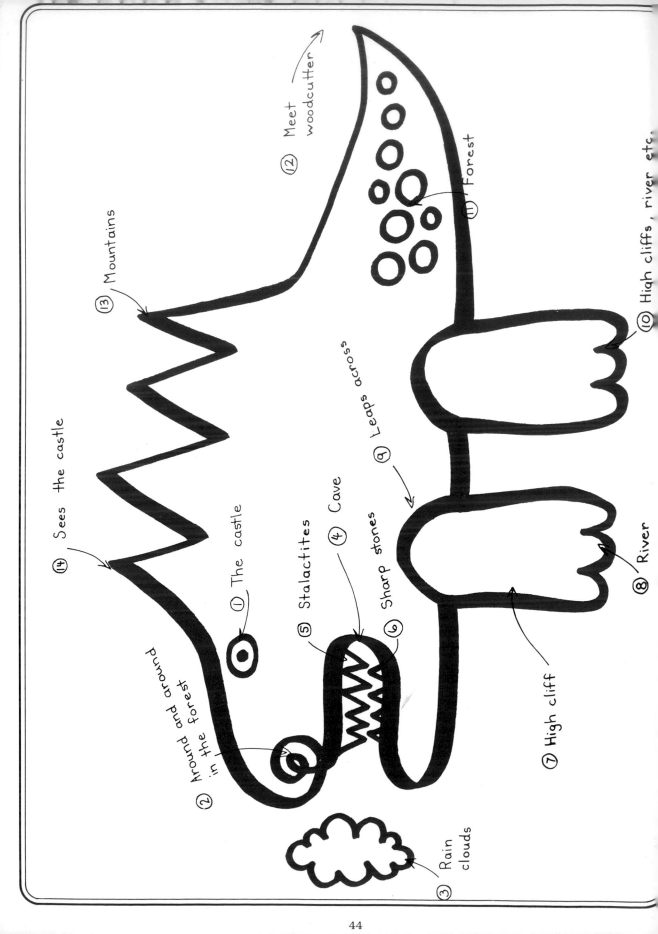

① The castle
② Around and around in the forest
③ Rain clouds
④ Cave
⑤ Stalactites
⑥ Sharp stones
⑦ High cliff
⑧ River
⑨ Leaps across
⑩ High cliffs, river etc.
⑪ Forest
⑫ Meet woodcutter
⑬ Mountains
⑭ Sees the castle

THE PRINCESS
AND THE CRITTER

Once upon a time, there was a princess who
was thoroughly sick and tired of hearing the
fearless knights who live in her father's
castle bragging about how they battled
fierce dragons every day of the week.

So one day Alexis — for that was her name
— packed a bag and set off herself to do
battle with a dragon.

She walked for a long time until she came
to a deep, dark forest. The trees in the forest
were close together, and the paths wound
this way and that, and soon Alexis was lost.

She wandered around and around.

The sky filled with clouds, and it started to
rain.

Alexis was getting soaked! She needed
shelter.

Luckily, she happened upon a cave.

The cave was dark, and it smelled damp and unpleasant. But it was better than the rain. Alexis went into the cave.

Stalactites hung from the ceiling. Sharp stones littered the floor.

Alexis stood just inside and watched the rain. Suddenly, she heard a noise behind her. She let out a little yell, and spun around to see a big friendly-looking critter smiling at her.

"Wet enough to drown a whale," said the critter.

When the rain stopped, Alexis and the critter, who was also lost, decided to travel on together.

By and by, they came to a deep gorge with a river running at the bottom.

"Now what?" said Alexis.

"Now what, is you climb up on my back," said the critter.

Alexis did as she was told, and with one mighty leap, the critter and the princess were on the other side.

They walked on for a while longer until they came to another deep gorge with another river running at the bottom.

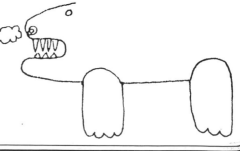

This time Alexis didn't say, "Now what?" She just climbed up onto the critter's back, and again, he leaped across with no effort whatsoever.

"Do you think we will ever find our way home?" Alexis said to the critter. They were walking by a thick woods. [*These are the trees growing in the woods.*]

"Let's ask that wood cutter if he knows where your castle is," said the critter.

So the princess and the critter approached the wood cutter who was sitting under a tree eating a simple lunch of bread and cheese.

"I have heard of a castle," he said. "A traveller told me once of a castle far across the mountains..."

He pointed to the west where Alexis could see high mountains standing against the sky.

"That MIGHT be my father's castle!" said Alexis.

"Only one way to find out," said the critter.

So they thanked the wood cutter and started out in the direction of the mountains.

They walked for a long time and finally came to the foot of the first mountain. Then for many days they climbed up one side and down the other, up one side and down the other, over mountain after mountain.

One day Alexis looked down and saw a valley far below, and in the valley was a castle.

"We're home!" she shouted.

The princess and the critter ran down the mountain.

Alexis burst excitedly into the room where the king and his knights were sitting around telling their dragon stories.

"You're back!" said one of the knights. "Did you battle a dragon, girl? Did you bring back the head for us to hang on the wall?"

He laughed and all the other knights laughed, "Ha! Ha! Ha!"

Alexis was too excited to care about their joke. "I didn't see any dragons," she said, "but I had a lot of good adventures, and I met a neat critter."

She went to the door and called the critter.

When the critter came into the room, all the knights, and even the king, started to shout, "A dragon! A dragon! Run for your lives!"

And that's what they did. They ran out the doors, they jumped out the windows, they hid in the cellar.

"What scared them?" asked Alexis.

Do you know?

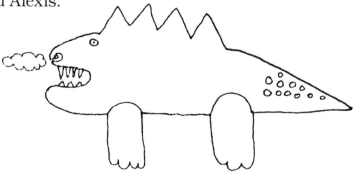

TELLING POINTS

1. There is a great temptation to say, "She let out a little yell and spun around to see — a big friendly DRAGON smiling at her." Make sure you say critter.

2. This figure takes lots of room to draw. If you do find yourself running out of room on the right, after the second deep gorge, remember that the dragon looks fine with his tail in the air.

THE FURTHER ADVENTURES OF
THE PRINCESS AND THE CRITTER

1. Name the princess after a friend. Who else might live in the castle with the princess? Give them names, too.

2. Add some markings on the dragon's belly — right after they cross the first gorge and before they get to the second — what are those? Add some markings to represent things that they came upon going over the mountains. Try making the dragon a winged dragon; can you work it into the story?

3. This dragon is a basic four-legged dragon, but what if it was, say, an eight- or ten-legged dragon? That's a lot of rivers to cross, but think of the adventures along the way!

4. Draw a picture of the princess' castle and the people who live there.

5. Draw your idea of what a dragon would look like.

6. On your own or in a group, list ways that Alexis is different from other princesses you have read about. Make another list of ways in which she is similar to those princesses.

7. Read THE PAPER BAG PRINCESS by Robert Munsch.

8. Find another story with a dragon and/or a princess and share it with the class.

9. Find out what a knight's job consisted of — besides slaying dragons.

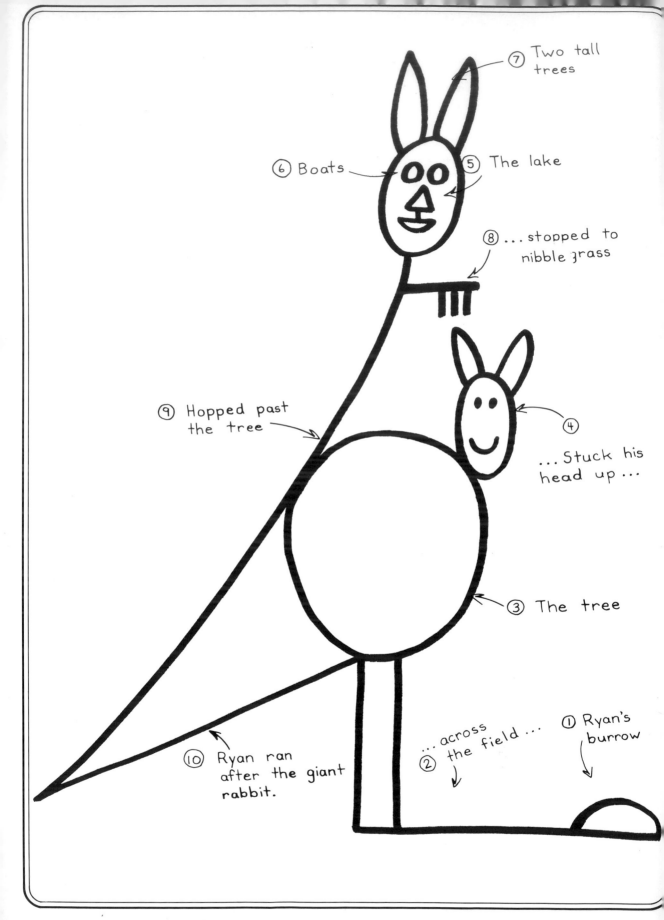

THE GIANT
RABBIT STORY

I'm not sure that this story is true, but my friend, Ryan Rabbit, told it to me, and he says it is. I'll tell it to you, and you can let me know what you think.

  One morning — according to Ryan — Ryan came out of his burrow...

...hopped across the field...

...and — this is one of the things I find hard to believe, but Ryan says he does it all the time — he climbed up to the top of the big tree that grows in the field, just to have a look around.

He stuck his head right up through the top
branches.

Away to the north he could see the lake
where two little boats and a big sailboat
were bobbing in the water. That would be
Mary's Lake. You've probably been there.
Do you remember those two big trees
growing at the end of the lake?

Then, right beside the lake — and if you thought that bit about a rabbit climbing a tree was hard to believe, wait till you hear this — he says he saw A GIANT RABBIT. It was brown and about two metres tall.

Suddenly, it started hopping toward the tree where Ryan was. Then, he says it hopped over and stopped to eat some grass. After a few nibbles...

...it came hopping right by the tree. Ryan said he called to the giant rabbit to stop, but it didn't.

Ryan jumped down from the tree and ran
after the giant rabbit, but he couldn't catch
him. He claims that rabbit could hop three
metres in one hop!

   That's his story...Oh, there was one other
thing; listen to this! He says that that giant
rabbit was carrying a BABY GIANT
RABBIT in his pocket! Can you believe that!

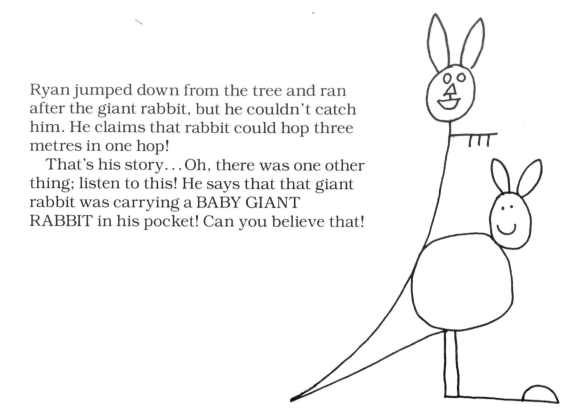

TELLING POINTS

1. The kangaroo takes up a lot of room; be sure to start your figure near the lower right hand corner of the drawing space.

THE FURTHER ADVENTURES OF THE GIANT RABBIT

1. This story revolves around a case of mistaken identity. Working alone or in a group, make a list of other cases where one animal could be mistakenly identified as another — for example, a lion that is mistaken for a giant kitten or a kitten that is mistaken for a miniature lion.

2. Can you think of your own story about a different case of "mistaken identity"?

3. Even if his story isn't true, Ryan is a remarkable rabbit. Brer Rabbit is another remarkable rabbit who appears in the Uncle Remus stories. Learn a Brer Rabbit story to share with the class.

4. Write a story about what would have happened if Ryan Rabbit had managed to catch up with the Giant Rabbit.

5. Find out everything you can about kangaroos and share your findings with the class.

6. On your own or in a group, make a list of ways that kangaroos and rabbits are similar and another list of ways in which they are different.

7. Make a list of famous rabbit characters from books, television and movies. Draw pictures of some of these characters.

8. Write a story about a race between a rabbit and a kangaroo.

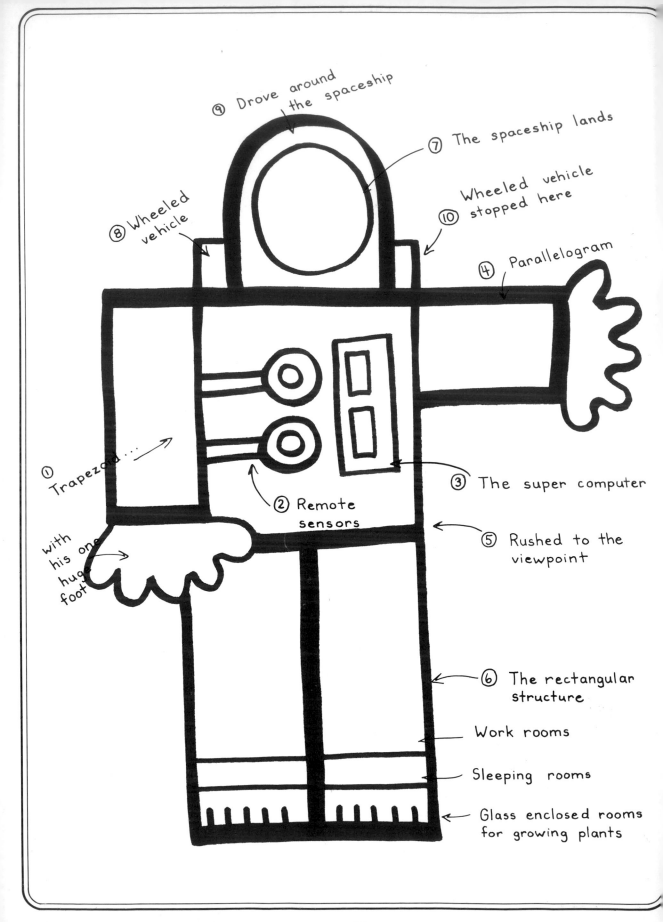

⑨ Drove around the spaceship

⑦ The spaceship lands

Wheeled vehicle stopped here

⑧ Wheeled vehicle

⑩

④ Parallelogram

① Trapezoid...

② Remote sensors

③ The super computer

with his one huge foot

⑤ Rushed to the viewpoint

⑥ The rectangular structure

Work rooms

Sleeping rooms

Glass enclosed rooms for growing plants

TRAPEZOID AND PARALLELOGRAM

This is Trapezoid, a rectangular solid from the planet Geo. Trapezoid was Captain of the interstellar exploration vehicle, Critical Angle, and his mission was to search the universe for other forms of intelligent life.

One day, as he was sitting at the view port of the ship, he spotted a barren asteroid. He didn't think there was much hope that such a dry bit of rock would have life on it, but....

...he deployed his remote sensors...

...and activated the super computer's search function.

Much to his surprise, the computer began to blink and whir frantically, indicating that it had found signs of life.

Trapezoid hopped on his one huge foot to where his friend, Parallelogram, had been resting in hyper-sleep for the last five hundred years.

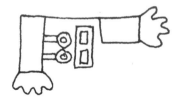

They rushed to the view port and looked out as the ship approached the asteroid.

The super computer whirred to life and printed out an analysis of the data it had collected.

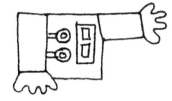

The alien life forms live in a rectangular structure — the computer said — that was divided into spaces for sleeping and working. At one end there were smaller rooms that were used to store supplies and two glass-enclosed rooms [here] where the aliens grew plants — presumably to eat.

Trapezoid piloted the ship to a smooth landing right next to the rectangular structure.

Almost immediately, a wheeled vehicle emerged from a door in the side of the rectangular structure.

It circled the ship and stopped [*here*]. One of the vehicle's doors swung open. A creature with a gleaming white skin stepped out of the vehicle and raised one arm in greeting.

"What do you think it is?" said Parallelogram.

"I have no idea," said Trapezoid. "But it is very strange."

What kind of a creature do you think it was?

THE FURTHER ADVENTURES OF
TRAPEZOID AND PARALLELOGRAM

1. Trapezoid and Parallelogram are just two examples of the kinds of creatures that live on the planet Geo. Draw pictures of some others. How do they move? How do they eat? How do they sense things? What might their names be (think of the names of some other geometric shapes)?

2. The story gives a very brief summary of the data analysis of the "rectangular structure". Report more fully on what life is like for the aliens on the "barren asteroid".

3. Assuming the "barren asteroid" is in this solar system, where do you think it might be?

4. Write a story about what happened next. Were Parallelogram and Trapezoid able to communicate with the "alien"? Was the "alien" friendly? What were they able to learn from each other?

5. Draw a picture of the inside of the interstellar exploration vehicle, Critical Angle.

6. Draw a picture or make a model of a "super computer". Write a paragraph telling what kinds of things you would expect your super computer to do for you. Compare lists.

7. On your own or in a group, make a list of geometric shapes. Draw the shapes and then try turning each into a space creature.

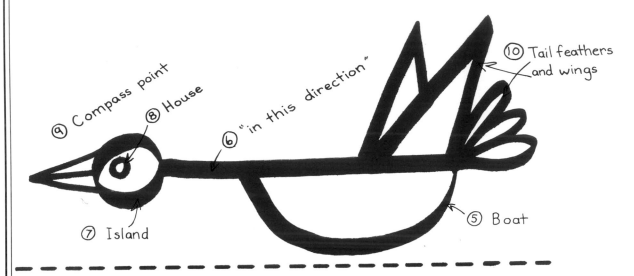

⑨ Compass point
⑧ House
⑥ "in this direction"
⑩ Tail feathers and wings
⑦ Island
⑤ Boat

② The letter "J"
③ Bicycle
④ Ocean
① Train track

Chug Chug Chug Chug Chug Chug

GOING TO MAROONAWOO

NOTE: For this story, besides a surface to draw on and something to draw with, you'll need a piece of white paper wide enough to cover the bottom half of the drawing — this is your snow. Have the paper at hand with pieces of tape on the upper corners ready to fix it in place over the drawing when it starts to snow in the story.

When it was time to leave for Maroonawoo, Conrad went to the railway station and bought a ticket. The train headed down the track, "Chug! chug! chug!"

When the train stopped at the end of the line, Conrad asked the conductor, "Are we in Maroonawoo?"

The conductor shook his head. "You silly goose!" he said. "This train doesn't go to Maroonawoo!"

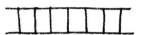

Outside the station, Conrad met a boy named James. [*James starts with the letter 'J'*]

James sold Conrad his bicycle and off he pedalled, heading — he hoped — for Maroonawoo.

Eventually, after days and days of pedalling, he reached the ocean.

He asked a fisherman, "Am I getting close to Maroonawoo?"

The fisherman looked at the bicycle and shook his head. "You silly goose!" he said. "You can't get to Maroonawoo on a bicycle. It's across the ocean!"

So Conrad sold the bicycle and used the money to buy a boat.

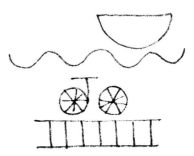

He set sail — he hoped — for Maroonawoo.
He sailed in this direction...

...until he reached an island. Conrad went
and knocked on the door of a small house
[*here*] and asked the old woman who lived
there if he was at Maroonawoo.

The old woman shook her head. "You silly
goose!" she said. "You're going the wrong
way. Maroonawoo is south, and you've been
sailing north. Let me show you!"

She took out a compass and showed Conrad
how the arrow pointed in the direction he
had been sailing. [*Like this.*]

"And compasses always point to the
north!"

Conrad asked if he might stay and rest for
the night before heading off again. The old
woman made him supper, and sent him to
bed.

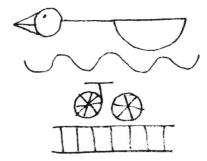

But in the middle of the night, the weather turned cold. Icebergs floated down from the Arctic and the ocean froze solid.

When Conrad woke up, he saw that his boat was stuck in the ice! And to make matters worse, it was starting to snow! The snow got deeper and deeper and deeper! And when it stopped there was snow all the way up to here.

"I'll never get to Maroonawoo now!" wailed Conrad. "My boat is stuck in the ice."

The old woman shook her head. "You silly goose!" she said. "Why don't you fly?"

"Hey! I never thought of that!" said Conrad. He unfurled his tail feather and spread his wings. With a flap and a honk, he was off!

The old woman shook her head as he disappeared from sight.

"What a silly goose!" she said.

TELLING POINTS

1. Keep the secret — don't say that the story is about a goose. The listener should wonder until the end whether the "silly goose" is a goose or a silly person.

2. Move the paper — the snow — up from the bottom of the drawing to indicate the snow getting deeper as you say, "got deeper and deeper and deeper...". Tape the paper in place to cover everything but the goose and continue with the story.

FURTHER ADVENTURES ON THE WAY
TO MAROONAWOO

1. Retell the story with your own or a friend's name. Make up names for all the people that the silly goose meets in his/her travels.

2. Before he gets to the ocean Conrad tries to get to Maroonawoo on a train and a bicycle. What other ways can you think of that he could travel? Add them to the story, remembering to keep your drawings very simple. Remember, too, that they must be in the half of the picture that will be covered by the "snow".

3. Maroonawoo is a made-up name. Look in the atlas and find names of real places in the south where Conrad might go. Find names for the places along the way where Conrad stops.

4. Learn to use a compass.

5. Make a treasure map using symbols or simple pictures to show the path. Put in directions — east, east, north, south — and challenge your friends to use a compass to find your treasure.

6. "Silly goose" is an expression. On your own or in a group, list other expressions that describe people using animal names.

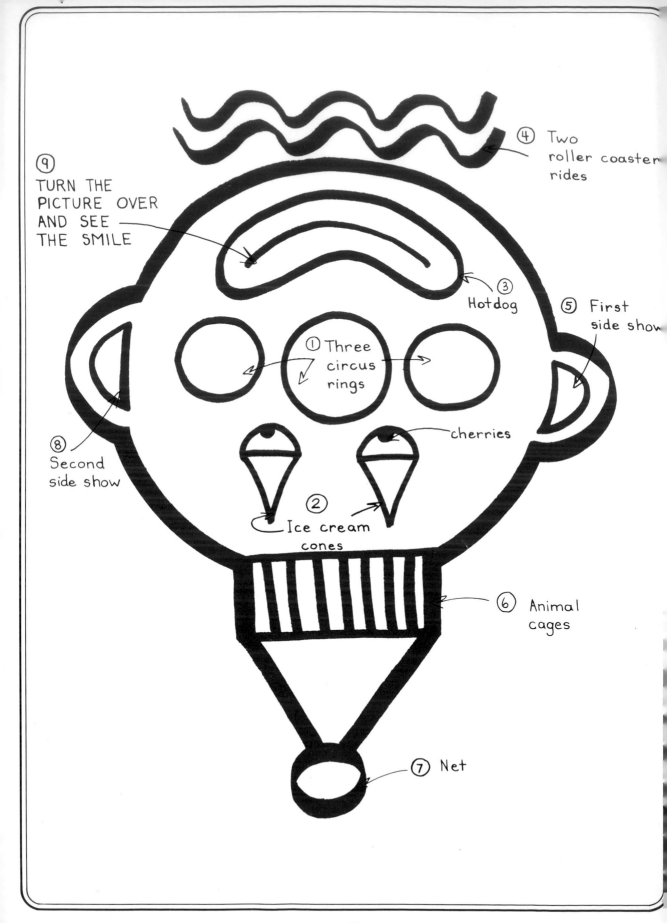

④ Two roller coaster rides

⑨ TURN THE PICTURE OVER AND SEE THE SMILE

③ Hotdog

⑤ First side show

① Three circus rings

cherries

⑧ Second side show

② Ice cream cones

⑥ Animal cages

⑦ Net

UNCLE BOB

NOTE: You will need to turn the drawing over at the end to see the finished picture. Do your drawing on a piece of paper on an easel or on a transparency on an overhead projector. Obviously, a blackboard won't work.

What a great circus! Rides and side shows and wild animals, cotton candy and hot dogs, and right in the middle of the whole thing, the tent with the three big rings [*right here*] where the performers would appear.

Uncle Bob had promised to meet Jesse and Aleisha there, but he was nowhere to be seen.

Waiting there and smelling all the good smells, Jesse and Aleisha started to feel hungry. They bought themselves two big ice cream cones, with cherries on the top.

Aleisha was still hungry, so she had a big hot dog, too.

When Aleisha had finished her hot dog and
Uncle Bob still wasn't there, Jesse
suggested a ride on the roller coaster.

Wheeee! Up and down and up and down
and up and down they went.

Aleisha was feeling a little bit sick, so
Jesse went again by herself.

"Hey Aleisha!" Up and down and up and
down and up and down. Aleisha couldn't
even watch.

"We'd better try to find Uncle Bob," Aleisha
said.

They walked over to a side show where a
man was swallowing swords. They looked
all around, but Uncle Bob wasn't there.

A little further on they came to the wild
animal cages. They were walking along
looking at all the animals when...

...the lion escaped! Jesse and Aleisha watched as the keeper and his helper ran after the lion, threw a net over him and dragged him back to his cage!

They spotted another side show where a woman in a tiger-skin suit was juggling flaming torches. They ran over and looked all around, but they couldn't see Uncle Bob anywhere.

Finally, they were back at the roller coaster ride again.

"It's almost time for the show!" said Jesse. "Where is Uncle Bob?!"

"Look!" cried Aleisha. "Is that him?"

A man dressed in a brightly colored suit
was coming toward them — walking on his
hands. When he got to the girls he did a flip
in the air and landed on his feet.

TURN THE
DRAWING
OVER

"Uncle Bob!" Jesse and Aleisha cried
together. "You're here!"

"I am, I am!" said Uncle Bob with a big
smile. "Are you ready for the show!"

He took them both by the hand and led
them into the big tent to watch the show as
his very special guests!

TELLING POINTS

1. This is another one of those stories where you have to flip the drawing at the end. You have to use a sheet of paper or a transparency, not a blackboard.

THE FURTHER ADVENTURES OF UNCLE BOB

1. Use your own name and the names of your friends in the story.

2. Working alone or in a group, make a list of other things that you might see in the two side shows. Use some of these ideas in retelling the story.

3. Give Uncle Bob some hair. Experiment with different ways of drawing the hair. How could you fit the hair into the story? Remember that when you draw the hair, the drawing will be upside down.

4. Try different designs for Uncle Bob's hat. How would the story change with a different hat? Remember that the drawing is upside down when you draw the hat.

5. On your own or with a partner, make a list of the tricks that Uncle Bob would do in his clown act.

6. Draw a picture of the flame swallower or one of the other acts in the circus.

7. Write a poem about a roller coaster.

8. How could you change the story by giving Uncle Bob a bow tie instead of a frilly collar?

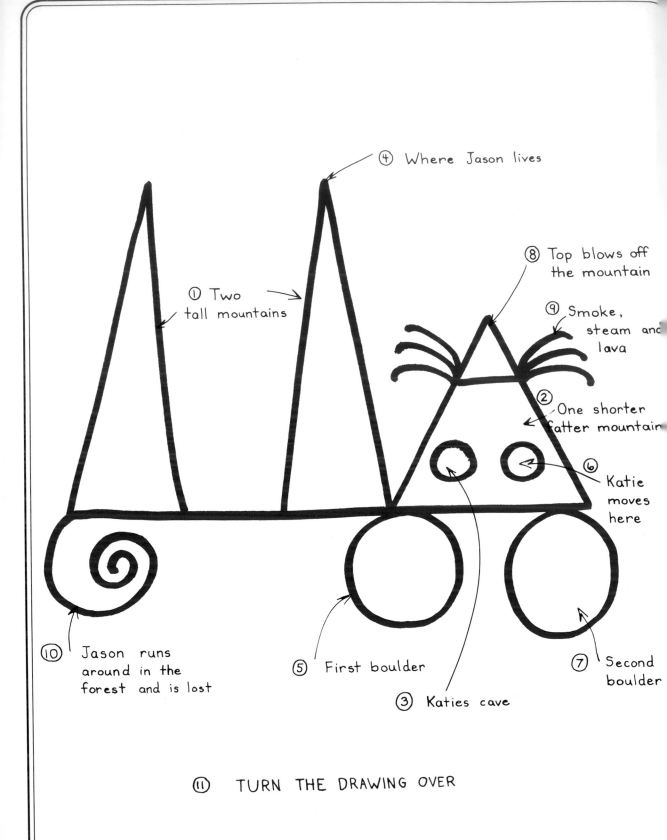

④ Where Jason lives

① Two tall mountains

⑧ Top blows off the mountain

⑨ Smoke, steam and lava

② One shorter fatter mountain

⑥ Katie moves here

⑩ Jason runs around in the forest and is lost

⑤ First boulder

③ Katies cave

⑦ Second boulder

⑪ TURN THE DRAWING OVER

KATIE AND THE GIANT

NOTE: You will need to turn the drawing over at the end to see the finished picture. Do your drawing on a piece of paper on an easel or on a transparency on an overhead projector. Obviously, a blackboard won't work.

You have no doubt heard of the three mountains in western Ontario called The Pointed Sisters.

Well, in case you haven't, I will tell you that those mountains looked something like this. There was one tall one here, another very tall one right next to it, and a third, that was not quite so tall as its two sisters.

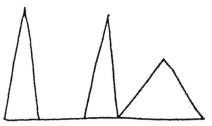

I would be surprised, though, if you had heard of Katie who lived in a little cave near the bottom of the third mountain.

And if you haven't heard of Katie, you almost certainly haven't heard of Jason who lived on the mountain next door...

Jason was a giant — a huge giant with legs as big as trees and shoulders like boulders.

In fact, the way Jason got such big shoulders was by lifting boulders. Every morning for at least two hours, he would exercise, picking up huge rocks and lifting them — UUUUNNNNH! — over his head.

And when he was feeling particularly strong, he would start throwing the boulders. They would go crashing down the mountain side making a terrible racket and shaking the ground for miles around.

One morning the noise of Jason's bouncing boulders woke Katie up and the shaking shook her right out of bed. But Katie set about her business, bravely trying to ignore the giant's game.

She had just gone outside and was starting to gather some flowers when — WHOMP! — a huge boulder landed right beside her [here].

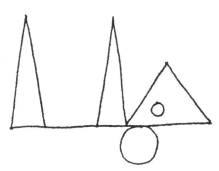

Katie was angry. She rushed to the bottom of Jason's mountain and yelled up at him: "Stop throwing those big rocks, you big galoot!"

The giant looked down at little Katie, and laughed: "HAR! HAR! HAR! Who's going to make me...you little galoot! HAR! HAR! HAR!"

Katie didn't have an answer for that question, so she went and packed up all her things and moved to another cave on the other side of the mountain...[here].

She thought she would be safe enough from flying boulders there, and for a while she was.

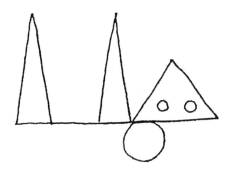

But as Jason lifted more and more boulders, he got stronger and stronger, until, when he threw them, they went sailing right OVER the nearby mountains.

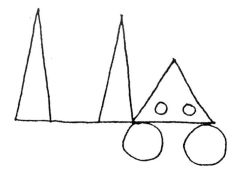

One day Katie and her friend, Jeremy, were playing near Katie's cave when — CRASH! — another giant boulder landed right between them.

Katie rushed around the rock to see if Jeremy was alright, and thank goodness he was. But Katie was mad!

She rushed right up the side of Jason's mountain and stood there shaking her fist at the giant.

"You just about hit my friend with your stupid boulder!" she yelled. "You better stop throwing things!"

"Or what?" laughed the giant. "HAR! HAR! HAR!"

"Or...." Katie was so mad she couldn't think of "or what". All she could do was stamp her foot really hard and yell: "I'm telling you — JUST STOP!"

At that moment, the whole mountain started to tremble and shake.

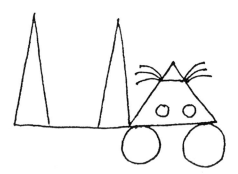

Katie and Jason watched in amazement as, below them, the whole top blew off Katie's mountain and lava and smoke and steam came pouring out.

The mountain gave another big shake and Katie went tumbling down the side and landed flat on her back.

Now, I don't know if it was Katie's stamping and yelling that caused that volcano to blow its top. Perhaps it was just ready to blow.

But Jason thought it was her stamping and yelling that did it.

"Wow!" he said. "If she can shake the top off a mountain just by stamping her foot, I'm getting out of here!"

And he ran down the side of this mountain, up the next mountain and down into the forest where he ran around and around till he was totally lost. He's still lost to this day.

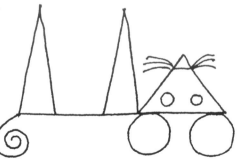

Meanwhile, at the bottom of the mountain, Katie picked herself up and got on her feet just in time to see Jason disappear over the next peak.

"Well, that scared him off," she thought.

TURN
PICTURE
OVER

She dusted herself off and said proudly, "Not bad for a mouse! Not bad at all!"

TELLING POINTS

1. Since you have to be able to flip the drawing at the end you need to use a large sheet of paper or an overhead transparency as your drawing surface — a black board is simply too heavy to flip.

2. Remember — DON'T mention who Katie is...

3. It is important to remember the part where Katie went tumbling down the mountain and landed on her back. That gets her upside down so that you can turn her back over at the end of the story.

THE FURTHER ADVENTURES OF KATIE AND JASON

1. Imagine how Jason and Katie would sound. Tell the story using their voices. You might want to remember to look WAY DOWN when you are Jason talking to Katie, and WAY UP when you are Katie talking to Jason.

2. "Act out" the story as you tell it. When Jason is doing his exercises pretend you are picking up a huge boulder. When you are telling about Katie stamping her feet and yelling, stamp your feet and yell.

3. There aren't really three mountains in Ontario called The Three Pointed Sisters. Look in an atlas and see if you can find three real mountains that might be the mountains in the story.

4. Use your own and friends' names in the story. You might want to add a few more friends to the part of the story where the second boulder comes crashing down.

5. Imagine what Katie's cave might look like inside. Write a description of it or draw a picture.

6. Katie obviously has a pretty hot temper. Write another story, not necessarily a draw-and-tell story where Katie's temper gets her into — or out of — trouble.

7. Draw a picture of Jason doing his exercises.

8. Find out how volcanoes erupt and share your findings with the class.

9. Is Katie's friend a mouse? Make a list of other animals he might be. Draw a picture of the two of them together.

10. Find other stories where a small creature outwits a larger one. Share one with the class.

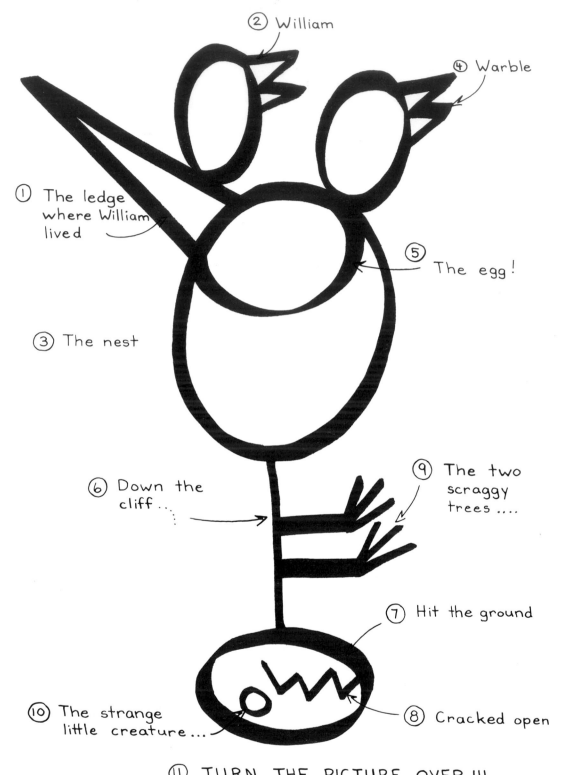

② William

④ Warble

① The ledge
where William
lived

⑤ The egg!

③ The nest

⑥ Down the
cliff...

⑨ The two
scraggy
trees ....

⑦ Hit the ground

⑧ Cracked open

⑩ The strange
little creature...

⑪ TURN THE PICTURE OVER !!!

WILLIAM AND WARBLE

NOTE: You will need to turn the drawing over at the end to see the finished picture. Do your drawing on a piece of paper on an easel or on a transparency on an overhead projector. Obviously, a blackboard won't work.

On a rocky ledge high on a cliff in the Badlands of Southern Alberta there lived a bird named William.

William spent most of his time hunting for worms. When he wasn't hunting, he was singing, hoping and wishing that another bird would hear his song and come to be his friend. And when he was neither hunting nor singing, he worked on his nest. He built it big just in case another bird came along to share it. And one day...

...another bird did come. [*She perched right here on the edge of the nest.*] Her name was Warble.

William and Warble discovered that they liked a lot of the same things — hunting for worms, singing, and nest building. They were very happy together.

The only thing they wished for was an egg, an egg that they could hatch into a chick of their very own. And then...

...one day William and Warble left the nest to go on a very long worm hunt. They didn't find any very long worms, but when they got back, they found something else — an egg — a huge egg just sitting there in the nest.

"A baby!" cried William, and he jumped up on that egg to keep it warm.

William and Warble took turns sitting on that egg for thirty-nine and a half days. And then, just before lunch of the fortieth day...

...the egg began to move.

"It's hatching! It's hatching!" hollered Warble.

The egg bounced around so much that Warble lost her balance and fell off. The egg bounced all around the nest and, finally, bounced over the edge and fell...down... down...down...

It hit the ground at the bottom of the cliff with a crack!

William and Warble flew down and perched on two scraggly trees that were growing out of the side of the cliff.

"Oh, Warble!" said William. "I can't look! What if our baby is hurt?"

"William!" cried Warble. "It's moving!"

And as they watched...

...the egg cracked open more. And a tiny creature crawled out and fell on its head.

"What is it?" said William.

"I don't know," said Warble. "But it's not very pretty."

"I don't think it's even a bird," said William.

"Well, it doesn't matter," said Warble bravely. "He's our baby, whatever he is. Come on!"

They flew down to the little creature, and when they got him turned right side up and had a look at him, they had to admit that, no, he wasn't very pretty and, no, he wasn't a baby bird.

He was a BABY DINOSAUR!

But William and Warble loved him anyway.

They brought him worms to eat, tons of worms, and...

Turn the picture over...

...pretty soon that little creature grew into a very large creature!

TELLING POINTS

1. Since you have to flip the drawing paper over to see the image at the end, you need to use a large sheet of paper or an overhead projector transparency to draw on — a blackboard doesn't work.

2. Your audience will probably call out, "It's a baby dinosaur!" as soon as you turn the picture over. If they do, simply echo it to confirm: "It was a BABY DINOSAUR!" If, after a moment, they haven't supplied the answer, then you go ahead and do it.

THE FURTHER ADVENTURES
OF WILLIAM AND WARBLE

1. The story says that William lived in the Badlands of Southern Alberta. The Badlands are a real place near a town called Drumheller. Find it on a map. See if you can find out what is special about the Badlands that makes it a likely place for this story to have happened.

2. If you can whistle, try making up a bit of a song for William to sing at the point in the story where you talk about him singing.

3. Working alone or in a group, make a list of the things that William and Warble did to amuse themselves during the thirty-nine and a half days that they were sitting on the egg. Share some of your ideas when you retell the story.

4. Working alone or in a group, make a list of names for William and Warble's new baby.

5. What special problems might William and Warble have to cope with as their baby grows up?

6. Working alone or in a group, make a list of other foods that the baby dinosaur could eat.

7. List the names of all the types of dinosaurs you know. What type is William and Warble's baby?

8. Make a list of other animals that might have hatched from the egg (a turtle, for example).

9. Make figures of William, Warble and the baby dinosaur out of clay or plasticene.

10. Write a story about what happened when it was time for William and Warble to fly south for the winter. Did they leave their baby behind? How did he manage? If he went south, how did he travel?

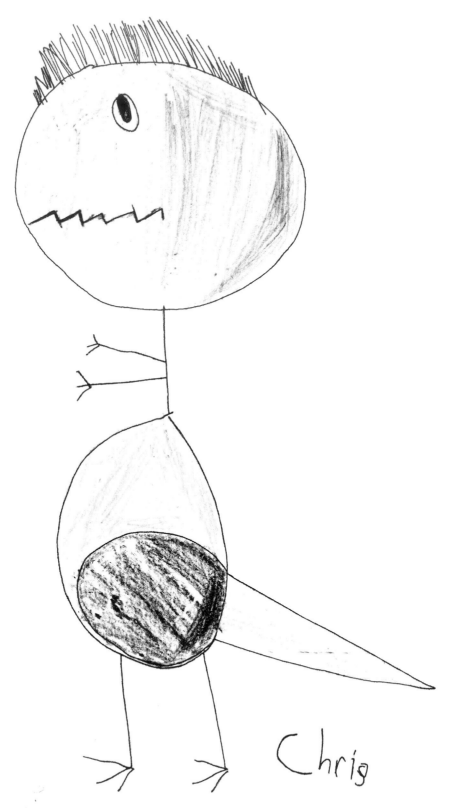

Chris